Contents

What to Do

Choose a face

Remember the colour you have chosen.

When you see your face on the page, you are the LEADER.

The LEADER reads the text in the speech bubbles.

There are extra words and questions to help you on the teacher's whiteboard. The LEADER reads these aloud.

When you see this stop sign, the LEADER reads it aloud.

STOP
My predictions were right/wrong because . . .

You might need:

- to look at the WORD HELP on pages 20–22;

- to look at the LOCATION HELP on page 23;

- an atlas.

If you are the **LEADER**, follow these steps:

1 PREDICT

Think about what is on the page.

- Say to your group:

"I am looking at this page and I think it is going to be about…"

- Tell your group:

"Read the page to yourselves."

2 CLARIFY

Talk about words and their meaning.

- Say to your group:

"Are there any words you don't know?"

"Is there anything else on the page you didn't understand?"

- Talk about the words and their meanings with your group.
- Read the whiteboard.

- Ask your group to find the LET'S CHECK word in the WORD HELP on pages 20–22. Ask them to read the meaning of the word aloud.

3 ASK QUESTIONS

Talk about how to find out more.

- Say to your group:

"Who has a question about what we have read?"

- Question starters are: how…, why…, when…, where…, what…, who…
- Read the question on the whiteboard and talk about it with your group.

4 SUMMARISE

Think about who and what the story was mainly about.

This page was mainly about
fact
fact

When you get to pages 16–17, you can talk to a partner or write and draw on your own.

  or

William's Dream

William lived in a small village called Wimbe. Most of the people in Wimbe live on small farms. They grow **crops**.

William was really interested in machines. He would take them **apart** and put them back together. He liked to find out how they worked.

William wanted to go to high school. He wanted to learn as much as he could. His dream was to learn how to help his family.

I am looking at this page and I think it is going to be about... because...

Are there any words you don't know?

Let's check: crops

Who has a question about what we have read?

How do you think William might help his family?

William

William went to this primary school in Wimbe.

This page was mainly about fact fact

STOP
My predictions were right/wrong because . . .

5

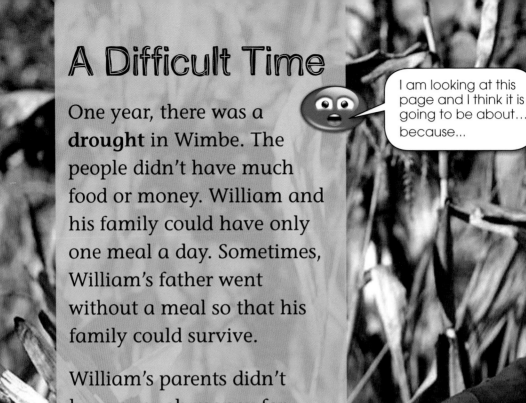

A Difficult Time

One year, there was a **drought** in Wimbe. The people didn't have much food or money. William and his family could have only one meal a day. Sometimes, William's father went without a meal so that his family could survive.

William's parents didn't have enough money for William to go to high school. They were worried. They knew how important school was and how good it would be for William.

I am looking at this page and I think it is going to be about... because...

Are there any words you don't know?

Let's check: drought

Who has a question about what we have read?

Why do you think people didn't have much food or money?

This woman's crop has **failed**.

STOP
My predictions were right/wrong because . . .

This page was mainly about fact fact

7

William's Idea

William couldn't speak or read English very well, but he liked books. He couldn't go to school. However, he could go to the library.

William was at the library one day when he saw a book with windmills on the cover. He knew that a windmill used wind to make **electricity**.

The book gave William an idea. There was a lot of wind in Wimbe. He would build a windmill!

I am looking at this page and I think it is going to be about... because...

Are there any words you don't know?

Let's check: electricity

Who has a question about what we have read?

How do you think William might start to build a windmill?

U·S·I·N·G

ENERGY

- Heat Energy Beyond Thermal
- Whichever Way the Wind Blows
- Thermal Energy—A Little Commodity

HENSIVE SCIENCE
ade 8

MACMILLAN

This is the book that gave William an idea.

This page was mainly about

fact

fact

STOP
My predictions were right/wrong because . . .

Solving Problems

I am looking at this page and I think it is going to be about... because...

William used a dictionary to work out the words he didn't know. He followed the **diagrams** in the book. He didn't have the tools he needed to build a windmill, so he made them!

William went to **scrapyards** to find what he needed. Some children laughed at him and said he was crazy! But that didn't stop William.

Are there any words you don't know?

Let's check: scrapyards

Who has a question about what we have read?

What have you learned about William from this page?

This is a close-up of one of William's windmills.

This page was mainly about fact fact

STOP
My predictions were right/wrong because . . .

From Old Junk to a Windmill

I am looking at this page and I think it is going to be about… because…

William and his friends found plastic pipes and a broken bicycle. They found an old **generator**, too. Then William made a windmill.

The people in his village laughed at him when he tried to put it up. However, the wind caught the **blades**. The blades spun faster and faster. Then the bicycle light he had attached came on. The laughing changed to **cheering**. William had made electricity.

Are there any words you don't know?

Let's check: generator

Who has a question about what we have read?

Why do you think the laughing changed to cheering?

William's father laughs outside their home. Their home now has electricity, thanks to William's windmills.

This page was mainly about fact fact

STOP
My predictions were right/wrong because . . .

A New Life for Wimbe

William's windmill changed the lives of the people of Wimbe. The women didn't have to walk for hours to get water. The windmill **pumped** the water for them and their crops. The homes in Wimbe had lights at night.

As for William, his dream had come true. He had **proved** that a small idea can grow into something big. You just have to keep trying.

I am looking at this page and I think it is going to be about... because...

Are there any words you don't know?

Let's check: proud

Who has a question about what we have read?

How might life have changed for William?

William's **proud** parents stand outside their well lit home.

This page was mainly about fact fact fact

STOP
My predictions were right/wrong because . . .

Something to Think About

 or

> There is no electricity at home.
> I can't...

Imagine life without electricity. How would life at home be different? What about life at school? Talk about your ideas with a partner, or write them down.

There is no electricity at school. We can't...

Do You Need to Find an Answer?

You could go to . . .

Library >

Expert >

Internet >

Do You Want to Find Out More?

You could look in books or on the internet. These key words could help you:

Malawi

Moving Windmills

William Kamkwamba

Wimbe, Malawi

windmills

wind power

Word Help

Dictionary

apart	into pieces or parts
blades	the long, thin, flat parts of a tool or machine
cheering	shouting to show happiness
crops	plants grown for food
diagrams	simple drawings that show how something works or the shape of something
drought	a long time without rain
electricity	power that moves along wires, used for giving light, heat and making machines work
failed	did not survive

generator	a machine that is used to turn energy into electricity
proud	very pleased with someone
proved	showed that an idea is true
pumped	pushed air or liquid into something
scrapyards	yards that have waste material

Word Help

Thesaurus

broken	damaged
crazy	foolish
idea	thought, plan
interested	attracted to, fascinated by
spun	turned, twisted
worried	concerned, anxious

Location Help

Where is William's Village?

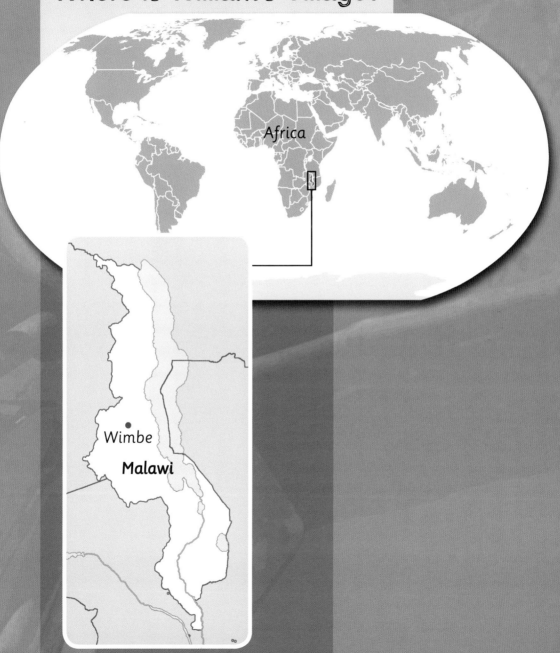

Africa

Wimbe

Malawi

Index